Emotional Literacy
and
Mental Health
in the Early Years

by
Dr Hannah Mortimer

A QEd Publication

Published in 2003

ISBN 1 898873 31 3

British Library Cataloguing
A catalogue record for this book is available from the British Library.

Published by QEd, The ROM Building, Eastern Avenue,
Lichfield, Staffs. WS13 6RN
Web site: www.qed.uk.com
Email: orders@qed.uk.com

Printed in the United Kingdom by Stowes (Stoke-on-Trent).

Contents

	Page
Introduction	5
Who this book is for	5
The importance of mental health	5
Promoting mental health in the early years	6
How to use this book	7
Chapter One – Emotional intelligence	8
Nurturing emotional intelligence in the early years	9
The importance of self-esteem and confidence	10
Chapter Two – When things go wrong	12
Developing social skills	12
Attachment Theory	13
Children whose self-esteem is low	14
Chapter Three – Early intervention projects	16
Starting early: PIPPIN Groups	16
Improving attachments: Hugs and Tugs	17
Joined-up approaches: Centres of Excellence	17
Providing a secure base: Nurture Groups	18
Parent training: NEWPIN	18
Reducing parental stress: RUMPUS Groups	19
Reducing risk: Sure Start	19
Chapter Four – Circle time	20
Using circle time to promote self-esteem	20
Meeting special educational needs	
and other disabilities	26
Circle time – have a go!	27

**Chapter Five – Supporting children with
emotional difficulties**   28
   Planning for children who have emotional difficulties   28
   Taking Early Years Action Plus   30

Chapter Six – Working in partnership with others   32
   The LEA   32
   The Health Service   33
   CAMHS   33
   Social Services   34

Chapter Seven – Listening to children   35

**Chapter Eight – Supporting young children
through life changes**   37
   Talking to young children about family breakdown   37
   Helping children through bereavement and loss   38
   Secure base   40

References   42

Useful resources   43

Organisations and support groups   45

Introduction

Who this book is for

This book will be useful for early years educators working in all kinds of early years settings: pre-schools, private nurseries, day nurseries and schools. It will also be helpful for individuals training on NVQ or pre-school diploma courses and of interest to childminders, parents and carers of children in their early years. In other words, it will be of interest to all those who live or work with children who are at the Foundation Stage of their education and who wish to support and nurture their emotional development.

The importance of mental health

The publication *Promoting Children's Mental Health within Early Years and School Settings* (DfES, 2001) was put together by the Department for Education and Skills (DfES) in conjunction with the Mental Health Foundation and the Advisory Group on emotional and behavioural difficulties. It forms guidance for local education authorities (LEAs), schools, early years settings and Child and Adolescent Mental Health Services.

It starts by defining 'mental health' as the ability to:
- develop psychologically, emotionally, intellectually and spiritually;
- initiate, develop and sustain mutually satisfying personal relationships;
- use and enjoy solitude;
- become aware of others and empathise with them;
- play and learn;
- develop a sense of right and wrong;
- resolve (face) problems and setbacks and learn from them.

The guidance goes on to describe and define mental health problems as experienced by children (such as 'attachment disorders' or 'conduct disorders') and links this back to the term 'emotional and behavioural difficulties', suggesting that the one has a greater risk of leading to the other. It stresses the link between emotional well-being and learning well. It also describes 'risk' and 'resilience' factors in children, families and communities, leading in to whole-school approaches to promoting children's mental health. In this book, you will read about the approaches you can take to promote mental health in the children you live and work with. Early years settings are also encouraged to do this through:

- stable childcare arrangements so that children interact with just a few primary caregivers in any one day;

- low staff turnover so that children are cared for by the same individuals over several years;

- good staff training in child development;

- adequate staff to child ratios;

- positive behaviour management.

Promoting mental health in the early years

The DfES guidance suggests that these are the main early interventions that professionals in early years settings can make, many of which are described in this book:

- home visiting, parent 'drop ins', courses run for parents in such areas as literacy and computing skills;

- parenting classes which enable parents to build on their strengths and learn new ways of engaging with their children;

- work with small groups of vulnerable children or vulnerable children individually around strategies to promote positive behaviour, social development and self-esteem;

- the teaching of interpersonal problem-solving skills to young children;

- compensatory nurturing experiences for vulnerable children.

In this book, you will find ideas for doing two things. You will be encouraged to think about how you can create the right ethos for encouraging *all* children's mental health during the early years. You will also consider some interventions you can make to support particularly vulnerable children.

How to use this book

In Chapter One, we will discuss the term 'emotional intelligence' and decide what this might 'look like' in early years. Two aspects of emotional intelligence are self-esteem and confidence and we will look at how these are closely bound into children's early learning and behaviour. In Chapter Two we will consider what happens when things go wrong, and decide what we mean by 'vulnerable' children and what compensatory approaches we might need to build in if we are to encourage their emotional well-being. Chapter Three describes some early intervention projects which early years workers have found particularly helpful, including the development of Nurture Groups, Sure Start schemes, work on early attachments, and positive approaches to behaviour management. One of these approaches is developed more fully in Chapter Four with ideas and suggestions for you to try out using circle time in an early years setting or house group.

Some children have emotional difficulties severe enough for their learning and play to be significantly affected. These are the children for whom you need something 'additional' and 'different' in your early years setting and they are therefore considered to have 'special educational needs'. Chapter Five provides ideas for supporting children with emotional difficulties in settings under the *SEN Code of Practice* (DfES, 2001). If it becomes necessary to involve other professionals, then Chapter Six describes who these might be and how you can work with them. Chapter Seven helps us think about how we can listen to young children and what their behaviour and words are telling us. Chapter Eight helps you to work preventatively and provides ideas for helping you understand and support children through major life changes such as family breakdown or bereavement. There are sections on useful resources and references at the end of the book.

Chapter One

Emotional intelligence

The term 'intelligence' has been considered controversial by many, mainly because it seems to imply that gifts such as cleverness are pre-programmed and unchangeable. Does 'intelligence' exist as a concept, or is it simply a measure of how a child performed on a particular assessment on a particular day? Is intelligence 'fixed' by genetic make-up, or does it alter with life's experiences and by what is learned and practised? Over time, environmental influences have been seen as having a significant impact on a child's intellectual development: it is not just what you are born with, it is the way you are taught and the experiences you have. Also, there is now a school of thought that claims that there are many different kinds of intelligences, all of which affect our abilities.

Researchers began to wonder whether we all had different intelligences in dealing with *emotions* as well as with knowledge and reasoning and the term 'emotional intelligence' began to emerge. This is a type of social intelligence that involves the ability to monitor one's own and other people's emotions, to discriminate among them, and to use the information to guide one's thinking and actions. Emotional intelligence is seen as involving self-awareness, the ability to manage emotions, self-motivation, empathy and relationship skills. Some would argue that these 'intelligences' are no more than 'social skills' that can be taught or learned through experience. Others have argued that they are ways to perceive and regulate emotional thought and some of us are better endowed than others.

In early years we need to be aware that some children find it genuinely more difficult than others to understand social situations and handle emotions. An understanding of the child's strengths and weaknesses in personal, social and emotional development should help us plan approaches for these children. The term 'emotional literacy' is sometimes used to describe the work we can do with children to foster their mental health and emotional intelligence. What might we see in the children whose 'emotional intelligence' is being nurtured successfully? This checklist will help you to understand the different strands to emotional intelligence and also help you to build on the children's strengths to improve their emotional literacy.

Nurturing emotional intelligence in the early years

- Can the children talk about the way they feel?

- Do the children have a number of words they can use to describe feelings?

- Can the children recognise when other people are happy/sad/angry/scared?

- Can the children recall past memories and the way they felt then?

- Do all the children enjoy and feel confident in their play?

- Can the children show friendliness and care towards each other?

- Can the children control their anger and frustration?

- Can the children use words and negotiations to solve disputes?

- Can the children play co-operatively with one another?

- If they are feeling anxious, are they reassured by a familiar adult or friend?

- Can each child wait just a little bit before his/her needs are met?

- Can each child initiate his/her own ideas and contribute in a familiar group?

- Can each child occupy him/herself when playing as well as playing with others?

- Is each child confident enough to try something new?

- Are the children beginning to be aware of right and wrong?

- Do the children feel able to make mistakes and learn from them?

- Are they able to 'take risks' in their learning, knowing that it is safe to fail?

The importance of self-esteem and confidence

Self-esteem and confidence are part of the wider picture of 'emotional literacy' and play a very important role in early learning. Children need confidence in order to face up to and cope with all the various challenges they will meet in their world. In the early years setting they will meet new people, new ways of playing, new activities, and if each of these is met and coped with successfully, they will develop more confidence for the next time. With each success comes a boost in self-esteem and self-respect – the children feel happy about themselves, and see themselves as valued members of the group. You can read more about the interplay between self-esteem, confidence and learning in *Personal, Social and Emotional Development of Children in the Early Years* (Mortimer, 2001b), also in this series.

How do confidence and social independence typically develop? The two-year-old is usually very dependent on a parent or carer and finds it difficult to separate unless the situation is very familiar. The young pre-school child may need to explore your group with Mum, Dad or a familiar carer there, even if they are in the next room. The older pre-school child can separate better, though might at first attach themselves to a particular helper or older child; this is absolutely normal. Sometimes a 'cuddly' or favourite toy is used to bridge the confidence gap until it is no longer felt to be needed.

Research tells us that children who have warm, affectionate relationships with their parents generally have high self-esteem. Children with a high self-esteem are more likely to view others positively too, and also to take a stand against discrimination and social injustice later on. Children with a high self-esteem are likely to be more independent, better socially adjusted and find it easier to learn.

Chapter Two

When things go wrong

Developing social skills

It sometimes helps if you can look at a young child's very emotional behaviour from the perspective of child development. If you can see the tearfulness or the tantrums as part and package (for whatever reason) of an immature emotional development, then this allows you to do something about it and to help the child develop new skills and confidences. It also gives *you* confidence: you are well used to handling the emotions of younger children and so you can now make use of your existing knowledge and expertise rather than feel you have something 'specialist' on your hands.

Young children arrive packed full of emotions. They experience intense feelings but do not yet have the words or experiences to make sense of these and cannot use words and negotiations to solve them. 'Emotional brain' and 'logical brain' are not yet in gear. The result can be an explosion of anger or grief which the child cannot control and which is also quite scary for all of you. It is no good asking the child 'why?' because they may neither know nor be able to put it into words. You are dealing with feelings and not logic. When children are in this state, they need to feel 'contained' (that you are in charge and that they are safe), they need to be calmed (rather than shouted at or aroused any more) and they need to feel that you still value them as people even if their behaviour is not appropriate. Other children also need to be protected from their emotions and behaviour. It often helps to have a quiet place to withdraw to until a child is calmed and until 'logical' brain begins to take over again and you can talk and play together.

You will see that the approach for handling emotionally driven behaviour is rather different from the approach for managing attention-seeking behaviour or willful 'naughtiness' and involves nurturing as well as managing. The use of positive approaches to behaviour management should provide you with the best framework. You can read more about this in the books *Developing Individual Behaviour Plans in Early Years Settings* (Mortimer, 2000b) and *Personal, Social and Emotional Development of Children in the Early Years* (Mortimer, 2001b). You will also find the *Curriculum Guidance for the Foundation Stage* (QCA, 2000) helpful since it provides you with the stepping stones and early learning goals which you should help the children reach by the time they have finished their reception year. You are provided with suggestions of what you should do as an adult in order to encourage each stage of the child's social and emotional development and so you can use this framework to teach and encourage children whose social and emotional development is immature.

Attachment Theory

There are some children whose challenging behaviour is very resistant to change. These are the children who can settle better if given 'secure attachment figures' to relate to in the nursery or playgroup; an interested key worker who can support, offer consistency of handling, and be there to reassure and encourage. 'Attachment Theory' argues that children develop a style of relating to important attachment figures in their lives, which secures for them the best parenting available under the circumstances. The study of attachments has opened up a whole new way of assessing family relationships and providing therapeutic support. The patterns of attachment remain remarkably consistent over time until the child is about six, and so can be observed, identified and worked with. Many of these parents find that their pre-school children are difficult to control, extremely angry and aggressive, or highly anxious and 'clingy'. Therapists might have tried to teach them behavioural management techniques, but where there is an attachment difficulty, the behaviour tends to persist, partly because the emotional climate and the relationships are not conducive to change.

Where attachment is working securely, an infant's cries and demands will be met reliably with sensitivity and warmth by the carer, and the growing child develops in confidence and independence. We know this because of the influential research of John Bowlby and colleagues into bonding, attachment and loss. If a parent is unresponsive or rejecting of their cries of distress, that child may act as if they are independent long before they are emotionally ready to be. They may pay little attention when their parent leaves them at nursery and seldom look at their parent or try to involve them in their play. This is known as a pattern of 'anxious-avoidant' attachment.

If a parent is inconsistent in his/her responses, perhaps because of periods of depression or frequent absences, the child learns to cry or shout louder with their demands, producing a pattern of 'ambivalent' attachment. There is also a pattern of 'disorganised' or 'controlling' attachment in which children develop a very controlling style over their parent in order to maintain some degree of predictability or structure in their lives. This pattern is common with parents who might have suffered loss, trauma or abuse themselves, or lack a 'secure base' of their own from which to provide nurture and care to others in their lives.

A general understanding of attachments does not mean that we should go forth and proclaim that a parent or child with whom we work 'has an attachment disorder'. However, it does help us to understand that there is an emotional component to the behaviour or the relationship which may involve us trying to intervene on an emotional level as well as a behavioural or teaching level. These are exactly the interventions that this book is helping you to think about in Chapter Three.

Children whose self-esteem is low

It is possible to identify children whose self-esteem is low. They tend to have a strong need for reassurance and praise from others with problems in trying out new experiences or in learning. They may seem insecure, lacking trust in their own competence, with a low opinion of themselves. People with low self-esteem sometimes have a negative, pessimistic approach to life and a sense of powerlessness. They can be reluctant to express opinions and have a tendency to overreact to failure. Adults and children with low self-esteem find it hard to evaluate their strengths and weaknesses objectively and to accept criticism without hostility or over-reaction. There is sometimes a negative, distrustful attitude to others, perhaps with a need to establish superiority or to bully. These are the children who need added support and encouragement in order to help them feel that they are successful in their play, learning and relationships. Circle time approaches (Chapter Four) have proved to be especially helpful for these children.

Chapter Three

Early intervention projects

There are many approaches that seem to foster personal, social and emotional development. These include the use of circle time, the development of nurture groups, work on early attachments and positive approaches to behaviour management. In this chapter, you will be introduced to a medley of these approaches. References or contacts for all of these approaches are given in *Special Needs and Early Years Provision* if you wish to study them in more depth.

Attachment Theory (introduced in the previous chapter) provides helpful pointers for early years educators in their work with children who have emotional and behavioural difficulties. If a child is to feel settled and confident enough to behave and to learn in a setting, educators need to invest time in building up trust, security, routine and consistency so that the setting becomes a 'secure base' for the child. It is also helpful to provide an 'attachment figure' for the child in the form of a warm, supportive and consistent key worker.

Starting early: PIPPIN Groups

The PIPPIN project (Parents in Partnership – Parent Infant Network) brings together mothers and fathers during the third trimester of pregnancy, seeking to provide the 'secure base' that was not sufficiently available to them during their own childhoods and is not present for them in their current relationships. They meet in a non-judgmental setting in which they can explore their feelings, deal with issues and learn more about their own relationships and patterns of behaviour. Though this can be a painful process, it can help them to understand better what are appropriate responses to their children in a particular situation. Parents who have attended the PIPPIN classes say that they are less anxious; less vulnerable to depression; enjoy their babies more; develop better relationships with their partner; and generally feel more confident, child-centred and skilled in coping with the ups and downs of family life.

Improving attachments: Hugs and Tugs

This kind of relationship playgroup is run regularly by Child and Family Service and Social Services Family Support Teams in several areas. For example, six mothers and children under six who have been identified as having attachment difficulties join a weekly group for 12 sessions. For the first hour, the mothers join a supportive counselling group with a clinical psychologist, a family support worker and a second psychologist who observes and provides feedback to the counsellors. While this is happening, the children play in a crèche. After sharing a drink together, everyone joins a circle for a series of finely graded relationship play activities which aim to gradually build up mother and child physical contact and enjoyment of each other. Mothers reported that the group had helped them feel closer to their children and more in control of things. They were able to share more pleasure and fun with their child and did not have to 'nag' all the time.

Joined-up approaches: Centres of Excellence

These are expected to exemplify how early education and childcare can be combined with a number of other services designed to support families (such as the teaching of parenting skills, family learning, adult basic skills) and to stimulate good practice by other providers in the surrounding area. Here is one example of a Centre of Excellence where the emotional welfare and self-esteem of the children, particularly those who are vulnerable, is paramount.

Many life events affect the families of children attending the community nursery at the Pen Green Centre of Excellence in Corby, Northamptonshire. By using semi-structured interviews with the parents, the staff have been able to keep up with these. For example, about a third of the children's families have been affected by change of job, major illness, separation or divorce. The children respond in many different ways to these changes. Some of them may appear withdrawn or full of grief, some may be angry and aggressive, some may be distractible or find it hard to relate to others, many find it hard to concentrate and many become needful of constant attention. The staff work hard to enhance these children's emotional well-being. They encourage close attachments to a key worker in the centre and they are also seeking to work creatively to support children through these changes.

Providing a secure base: Nurture Groups

These were developed 30 years ago in the Hackney area of London by psychologist Marjorie Boxhall. As an approach, it has been shown to reduce the number of children excluded from schools on account of their behaviour. The groups attempt to replicate a form of 'family life' based on intense personal interest and positive support from the teacher or classroom assistant. Each child is helped to feel special and valued. There are shared meals, and an emphasis on early sensory play and familiarity. Outings are arranged with parents and there are 'coffee days' for parents to come in and share notes about their children.

Parent training: NEWPIN

NEWPIN is a national voluntary organisation that helps parents under stress break the cycle of destructive family behaviour. Through a network of local centres, expectant mothers, parents, carers and children are offered a unique opportunity to achieve positive changes in their lives and relationships based on respect, support, equality and empathy. There are training programmes in parenting skills, family play, attachment and befriending skills and learning for life. There is support for mothers with depression and other forms of mental distress. One of the principle aims is to prevent emotional abuse.

Families can refer themselves in or be encouraged to attend by professionals. For the adults, NEWPIN offers an initial home visit, befriending, a 24-hour telephone support network, play sessions with the children, training for personal development, and therapeutic group or individual work. For the children, there is a safe, caring and stimulating environment away from family turmoil with opportunities for developing play and learning with their parent or carer, perhaps for the first time. Some centres are now developing fathers' groups too. The national contact address is given on page 46.

Reducing parental stress: RUMPUS Groups

These 'RUMPUS' (aRe yoU Mas and Pas Under Stress?) groups are run by an educational psychologist and a team of community health visitors in local health centres. The groups aim to support young parents and their early years children where there are particular difficulties in managing behaviour. A combination of approaches has been developed by the team to put parents at their ease, improve the attention skills of the children, encourage early language and lap play, build up family relationships and provide practical advice based on realistic expectations and week-by-week management of behaviour. Parents also make their own plans for encouraging positive behaviour in their children in a supportive atmosphere that aims to enable and empower rather than to prescribe.

Reducing risk: Sure Start

Sure Start is a cross-departmental Government initiative aimed at children under three years old and their families in a small targeted area of disadvantage. It concentrates additional resources and additional services in this tightly defined area in order to achieve seamless provision of preventative services. It involves all aspects of their lives including their health, education, social and leisure time. It brings together many different agencies and organisations in the statutory, private and voluntary sectors aiming to break down barriers and ensure coordinated and 'joined up' provision. Many of you will know of, or be working with, a local Sure Start scheme.

The Sure Start initiative is based on what we know from current research including what we know about early attachments and early emotional development. A review of research on prevention and early intervention concluded that there were four groups of protective factors that helped children in adverse conditions achieve good outcomes. These were an adequate standard of living, temperaments or dispositions that attract and encourage caregiving, dependable caregivers and networks of community support. Sure Start is, therefore, grounded in evidence from child development and attachment theory, as well as what works in supporting parents and young children within local communities.

Chapter Four

Circle time

Using circle time to promote self-esteem

Circle time is an ideal opportunity to bring many members of the group together to share their play and learning with each other. Within the circle, children learn to look, listen and learn from each other, and develop an identity with the rest of the group. The use of circle time activities in developing children's self-esteem and confidence is now well established. Circle time can be used for activities that children and adults can enjoy within a circle across all learning areas, from language and literacy through to creative development. You will find practical ideas for this in *Learning through Play: Circle Time* (Mortimer, 1998). For example:

Language, literacy and communication

Circle time can be an excellent opportunity to develop attentive listening, share experiences and respond to rhyme and story. Children can begin to associate sounds with patterns in rhymes and to develop confidence in expressing themselves through word games and discussion.

Magic wands

In this game, children can develop confidence while enjoying role play. You need a sparkly, magic wand. For all these activities, gather the children in a circle sitting on the floor.

Tell the children that you are going to play a 'pretend' game. You are going to wave a magic wand and you would like them all to pretend to be babies. When you clap your hands, they should stop pretending and be themselves again. Have a practice, changing them into babies and then cats. Then invite each child to think of something they would really like to be: a pop star, a puppy, a fireman, a giant, a lion etc. Wave your magic wand and 'change' all of the children into whatever it is they have chosen. Give each child a turn in choosing what the group should become.

Train game

Choosing activities that are great fun allows children to learn about language at the same time as developing confidence and motivation. Tell the children that you are going to eat a very funny dinner on a train. Invite the children to move their arms like the pistons of a heavy steam train, repeating everything you say. Chant this rhythm together: Coffee (four times); cheese and biscuits (four times); chocolate pudding (four times); bangers and mash (four times); SOOOOOUP!

Start the rhythm of this chant slowly, and gradually build up speed and momentum until the final 'soup' sounds like the whistle of the train. Finish by talking about journeys and visits.

Mathematics

Early counting skills can be practised in a fun and non-threatening way within the circle. Games involving position and space can help to develop early mathematical language, and there are opportunities for exploring number rhymes, songs and stories.

Three green jellyfish

You can help to develop confidence in mathematics by choosing circle games that are fun and that encourage early counting and number skills. For this game, you need a large tambourine.

Ask the children to wobble like a jelly. Tell them to shake all over when your tambourine shakes and stop when you beat it. Have two or three goes until the children are fully relaxed and attentive. Praise the children as they look and listen. Now tell the children you are going to sing a song about three jellyfish. Ask them to count to three with you. Encourage them to shake like a jelly each time they sing *jellyfish*. This rhyme can be sung to the tune of *Three Blind Mice*.

Three green jellyfish (twice),
Sat upon a rock (twice),
The first one felt like a swim, you know,
And slithered away to the sea, you know,
And left the rest on their own-i-o,
Just two green jellyfish.

Raise your hands in the air and wobble them down all the way to the sea for the 'slither'ing. Repeat one more time until there is one jellyfish left on the rock.

Colourful circles

Teaching early number skills also involves helping children identify and sort colours into sets. For this activity, you need four large hoops, coloured red, green, blue and yellow. Collect together a box full of small toys and objects, all of which are coloured a shade of red, green, blue or yellow. Try to have four or five toys per child.
Set the four hoops in the centre of the circle on the floor. Pass round the box and invite each child to put in their hands and pull out a toy without looking. Help the child place it into the hoop that has the same colour. Pass the box around until all the toys have been taken out and matched.

Personal, social and emotional development

Circles provide an ideal setting for sharing and turn-taking. Children learn to feel comfortable within the routines of circle time and to know what is expected of them. They are able to help and support each other through their ideas and actions, and to share a range of responses and feelings arising from the activities.

Passing smiles

This game helps children recognise and copy facial expressions. Make a smiling face. Ask the children if they think you are happy or sad. Make a frowning face. Ask the children how you look now. Try a surprised face and a sad face. Now look worried or frightened. Talk about feelings and faces, and invite the children to copy each expression that you make.
Now tell the children that you are going to play a game. You are going to pass a smile all the way round the circle. First smile at your neighbour and encourage a smile back. Then encourage that child to pass the smile to the next child until that child smiles back. Gradually pass the smile all the way round the circle. You can repeat this for

different expressions, passing a sad face, a cross face or a frightened face round. Finish with passing a smile again.

How do you do?
Call one of your helpers over. Shake hands and say, 'How do you do? I'm (your own name). What's your name?'
Ask the children why grown-ups sometimes shake hands. Talk about greetings in different cultures: a hug, a kiss on the cheek, a bow. Now practise shaking hands in the circle, by passing a handshake all around the ring. Finish by singing a song as you all shake hands together in a circle. It goes to the tune of *Here we go round the mulberry bush*.

This is the way we shake our hands
shake our hands
shake our hands.
This is the way we shake our hands
saying 'How do you do?' in the morning.

Knowledge and understanding of the world
Circle times can be talking times for many topics of interest. Children can talk about their worlds, their families and their communities. They can explore their worlds through songs and rhymes and explore features of living things through animal games.

Old Macdonald's zoo
You can use a musical circle time to introduce animal sounds and actions. Find out about the country of origin, habitat and diets of familiar zoo animals.
Tell the children that you are going to sing a song about Old Macdonald's zoo, and warn them that you are going to ask them soon for ideas of the animals that Old Macdonald might keep in a zoo:

Old Macdonald had a zoo
$E - I - E - I - O$
And in that zoo, he had a ...

At this point, stop the song and seek suggestions from the children. Accept one child's idea, and then ask the whole group for ideas for an action and a sound to go with that zoo animal, perhaps a 'tiger':

With a roar roar here
and a roar roar there
here a roar, there a roar,
everywhere a roar roar,
Old Macdonald had a zoo
E – I – E – I – O.

Continue for several verses, choosing a new child's suggestion for each verse.

Treasure chest
In this game, children explore a selection of made and natural objects. You need a large box, if possible looking like a treasure chest and a selection of made and natural objects, so that there is at least one per child. These might include a piece of pottery, a piece of driftwood, a feather, a small painting in a frame, a string of beads, an interesting stone, a fossil, a piece of shiny or colourful fabric. Have an equal number of natural and made objects, and make sure each one is interesting to feel, look at, listen to or smell. Place all the objects together in the box and close the lid until you are ready.
Invite each child in turn to take one object out of the treasure chest and to pass it around the circle so that each child can explore it. Now ask the children to tell you as much as they can about it. Talk about whether the object has been made by someone, or whether it is part of nature. Put that object to one side. Continue until each child has had a turn at choosing the object.

Physical development
Within the circle, children can learn to move confidently and with imagination. Action rhymes and rhythm games provide opportunities for practising many fine and large movements and teach the skills of watching

and copying others. Small toys and musical instruments can be handled and passed, each child inspiring the confidence of the next.

Merrily we roll along

You will need a large ball to roll and catch. Gather the children in a circle sitting on the floor with their legs in a V-shape in front of them. Call each child's name as you roll the ball to them and invite them to roll it back to you. When they are rolling and catching with confidence, ask each child to roll it to another by name: 'Tara, please roll the ball to Damien' etc. When you are sure that the children know each other's names, invite the children to call out another child's name as they roll the ball in their direction. Continue until everyone has had a turn of rolling and catching.

Copy cats

You will need a cassette or CD player and some rhythmic music. Gather the children in a circle, standing on the floor. Ask the children to listen for the music and then copy what you do. Ask for the music to be started and choose an action to do, such as rubbing your tummy, for the children to copy. Stop the music and ask the children to think of their own actions for everyone else to copy. Repeat the music while the children take turns to be the leader.

Creative development

Circles provide good opportunities for hatching and sharing good ideas. Children can explore sounds and movements and respond in a variety of ways to what they see, hear, smell, touch and feel. The opportunities for using music and dance within the circle are many.

Join the band

You need a selection of musical percussion instruments in a box or tray where they can be easily seen and selected. Place the box of instruments in the centre of the circle. Invite each child to come and choose an instrument for themselves. Invite the children to watch you: 'When I point to you, play your instrument.' Move your finger round the circle, using your face and your expressions to encourage the children to join in as you point. 'When I do this, stop playing your instrument.' Make a halt sign to each child in turn and encourage them as they stop playing. Once the children are used to the hand signals, you can use them to bring in different sounds at different times. Sit children with the same instrument together, so that you can use your signals to bring in whole sections of the 'orchestra' at once.

Smell and tell
Collect identical clear plastic containers with lids which you can keep on until you are ready to smell. Each should have a different fragrance in. Think up your own ideas of fragrances which the children will be familiar with, for example, perfume, vinegar, spice, tomato ketchup, honey, drinking chocolate. Cover the outside of the jars with paper so that they all look alike and arrange them on a tray. Talk about smells together and introduce your smelling bottles. Pass each one round in turn to be smelt. Allow each child to hold it so that they are in control, and allow children to be passed by if they are anxious. Talk about the smells and see whether the children can identify what any of them are.

Meeting special educational needs and other disabilities

Circle time activities are already widely used for helping children with special educational needs (SEN) to look, listen and feel a valued member of a group. It provides a useful way of providing activities that are inclusive for all children regardless of their special needs or previous experiences. Make sure that any child with particular needs has an adult helper close by if needed, and ensure that the helper knows what you are hoping the child will achieve from the activity. This might be a particular teaching target from the child's individual education plan (IEP), or it might be a more general goal such as helping the child to feel confident in a large group, or encouraging attention. The adult should help to direct the child's attention and use praise and encouragement to let the child feel successful. You will find many resources for circle time on page 43 and the *Music Makers Approach* (Mortimer, 2000a) is especially designed to include children in their early years who have SEN.

Circle time – have a go!

Here are some simple examples. Gather the children in a circle, sitting on the floor.

Favourite toys

Each child says what his or her favourite toy is. Everyone else makes it feel like a really good idea.

Animal friends

Each child thinks of an animal he or she would like to be, and chooses another child to be an animal friend. Then wave a wand and both children 'become' the animal for a little while.

Happy thoughts

Hold up your hand and say you are going to pass a happy thought all around the circle. Blow gently into your palm and with carefully cupped hands, pass it gently into the palms of the next child. Pass it all around the group, and thank the children for passing it back so gently.

Introductions

Help each child to introduce his or her neighbour around the circle and say one thing about them that they like, for example, 'This is Ahmed, and I like his smile.'

Touch and pass

Try to pass different touches around the circle. First touch palms, then fingertips, or elbows, or toes.

Treasures

Help each child to bring something they really treasure and show it to the others in the circle.

Musical teddy

This is a variation of 'Pass the Parcel', and excellent for less confident children who may wish to join in only passively. Pass teddy around the circle until the music stops. Then pretend that teddy 'talks' to the child holding it, making friends.

Chapter Five

Supporting children with emotional difficulties

Planning for children who have emotional difficulties

Each early years setting that is registered with the Early Years Childcare and Development Partnership (EYCDP) will have one person designated to co-ordinate the special educational needs in that setting. This special educational needs co-ordinator (SENCO) should take the lead in assessing a child's strengths and weaknesses when it is felt that the child might have SEN. You might find the book *The Observation and Assessment of Children in the Early Years* (Mortimer, 2001a) a useful tool here. Many practitioners now use the framework *Curriculum Guidance for the Foundation Stage* (QCA, 2000) to help them do this, identifying stepping stones or achievements which the child has reached in each area of learning and pointing out early learning goals or stepping stones still to be achieved. The stepping stones for personal, social and emotional development would be especially helpful when planning for children who have emotional difficulties.

The *SEN Code of Practice* (DfES, 2001) states that when a practitioner who works day-to-day with a child or the SENCO identifies a child with SEN, they should plan interventions that are *additional to* or *different from* those provided by the setting's usual range of strategies or curriculum. The SENCO must therefore work closely with colleagues to plan effective strategies and to monitor how these are making a difference for the child. The interventions to be used are recorded on an individual education plan (sometimes called an 'individual behaviour plan' for children with behavioural and emotional difficulties). Typical interventions might include the following, though in an inclusive setting many of these approaches would be available to all the children who may need support:

- Flexible start or finish times so that a child and parent/carer can avoid the usual rough and tumble and have a chance to settle in earlier or later than the other children.

- The appointment of a key worker to act as a 'secure base' for the child, supporting their play and keeping a watchful eye on their emotional needs.

- Work and play in small groups to help a child feel less socially 'overloaded' and more secure.

- The use of positive behavioural approaches to encourage more appropriate behaviour. You will find *Developing Individual Behaviour Plans in Early Years Settings* (Mortimer, 2000b) helpful.

- The teaching of social skills – including how to play with a friend and how to resolve conflicts.

- A 'quiet place' to withdraw to when things seem too much. Sometimes these areas have comfortable cushions, gentle light displays or even massage.

- Plans to provide extra nurturing and to allow the child to express feelings through sensory play.

The 'additional' and 'different' approaches will involve careful record keeping. The pupil record or profile for a child with SEN should contain information about the child's progress from the setting, from parents and from other services and professionals. These records are usually kept by the SENCO. The records should also include the child's own perceptions and views of their difficulties and their progress. This might be through photographic records of the child's enjoyment and successes, through records of things they have said, and through examples of their work and creations.

When a practitioner or SENCO identifies a child with SEN and plans interventions that are *additional to* or *different from* those provided by the setting's usual range of strategies or curriculum, this is known as taking 'Early Years Action'.

Taking Early Years Action Plus

Sometimes the additional or different approaches planned by a setting are not sufficient to help a child make progress in their emotional development. This is not surprising given the many reasons why children might be vulnerable, many of which go far beyond the setting itself. In these cases, the SENCO might make a referral to another agency or professional in order to have more guidance and support. This must be done in partnership with the parents and carers. For children who have emotional difficulties, close liaison with parents, carers or Social Services becomes very important. While you can work to alleviate difficulties in the setting, it could be that the child needs support and approaches within the home as well if they are to be helped in the longer term.

Communicating with families about emotionally vulnerable children can arouse all kinds of emotions in itself. Parents and carers can quickly become 'prickly' if they feel that you are criticising their parenting or if their own self-esteem is low. Try to understand why a parent might be saying something and listen to the emotions as well as the words. If they are expressing anger towards you, then it could be that they are feeling angry at themselves as well. Try to remain professionally supportive and emotionally objective so that you do not take things personally. If parents are avoiding the idea that there might be difficulties for their child, take time to share the good news of progress before you need to share the challenges. Give clear information about your expectations in order to *inform* a parent about what you hope to achieve at each age and stage. This will lead on to what you are going to plan together for those areas that are showing a weakness.

Try to involve parents and carers in the early years sessions wherever possible so they can see what you are trying to achieve. Rather than just sharing your approaches, share the reasoning behind them and an idea of how children typically progress in their emotional development. Try to share some of your enthusiasm in the way children play and learn and try to pass on skills. For helpless or troubled parents, try to give *practical*, workable advice, but avoid giving the impression that you are the successful ones and parents are failing; this can lead to resentfulness and avoidance. If a parent will not stop to talk, negotiate a home visit to meet on their territory. Start with establishing *their* views and feelings; this gives you important information about their value judgements which will help you decide how to introduce your own concerns. Listen first – talk later – find the common ground last. The 'common ground' is usually your mutual like of their child who is 'special' to both of you.

Some parents may appear overanxious. Take their views seriously and reassure them point by point with concrete evidence wherever possible. Some parents might realise there is a problem, but refuse any kind of outside help, even though you are convinced that things have come to that stage. Try explaining that it is *you yourselves* who need support and guidance from an outsider in order for you to provide the best support and help for their child.

Quite often in these cases, the outside support will come through the Health Service rather than the school support services. The parents or carers might have gone to their GP or health visitor and requested a referral to an NHS service. Another route for outside help might have come through Social Services, either as a result of a family needing Family Support, or because of concerns related to Child Protection or being on the 'at risk' register for child abuse. The various professionals who might be involved are given in the next chapter. Sometimes it is possible for the SENCO to work closely with the outside professional or agency to provide support for the child with SEN.

Chapter Six

Working in partnership with others

In this chapter, we focus on the outside professionals who might be advising and supporting you and the child who has emotional difficulties through Early Years Action Plus. Usually, these professionals will work for the Health Service CAMHS (mental health) team or the LEA. Sometimes you might be working alongside colleagues from Social Services or a professional or support volunteer from a voluntary organisation such as the NSPCC or Barnardo's.

The LEA

Each LEA has its own way of organising its support services and you will need to find out who the professionals are in your area and how you access them when you are putting together your SEN Policy. Some LEAs have general support services available to children from the early years through to age 19. More and more are developing early years support services in conjunction with the Early Years Childcare and Development Partnership or Behaviour Support Services in conjunction with their Pupil Support Services. If that is the case for you, there is probably a named early years support teacher, behaviour support teacher and educational psychologist for your area. Sometimes they work in a consultative way, discussing the child's difficulties and needs with you and the carers and helping you develop strategies for supporting the child. Education social workers (who work for the LEA and not the Social Services Department) can also play a helpful role in supporting families and helping better attendance. If a child is being statutorily assessed (because their special educational needs are so significant that it is felt that a Statement of SEN might be necessary) then there will also be a Parent Partnership Officer to guide parents and carers through the process. They can also put parents of a child with SEN in touch with an Independent Parent Supporter as an ally.

The Health Service

All children should have access to a health visitor and this person can be a useful source of information when a child first joins you, particularly if there are emotional difficulties, a history of abuse or being 'at risk', major life changes or family difficulties. If you work in a setting attached to a school, then there might also be a school nurse who can help. Sometimes the child and family might be referred to a Primary Mental Health Worker or a Child and Family Team where a team of professionals can work with the family in a number of ways. Counselling and advice might be on offer, family therapy or play therapy, and sometimes home visiting support. Often, there is a clinical child psychologist available to assess and advise on the child's general development and emotional needs. Some of these people work exclusively with children who have behavioural or emotional difficulties. Some work in family therapy teams or provide play therapy or art therapy for those children who are struggling to make sense of their lives or feelings.

CAMHS

These teams of professionals are all part of your local multidisciplinary CAMHS (Child and Adult Mental Health Services). In many areas, these services have been organised into four different tiers. Tier One includes services available to anyone through GPs, health visitors, school nurses, social services, voluntary agencies, teachers etc. These professionals are non-specialist and help to identify and offer general advice and preventative work on mental health. Tier Two is a level of service provided by one professional group who relate to each other through a network rather than a team. These might be clinical child psychologists, community paediatricians, educational psychologists or community psychiatric nurses. All are specialists in working with mental health. At Tier Three, a child might be referred to a specialist multidisciplinary team who work together to support more complex difficulties. Tier Four is rarely needed but includes highly specialised regional teams and centres, and in-patient facilities.

Social Services

Some children may be known to Social Services and you might find that there is a named social worker or family support worker. Sometimes, the family support worker works with parents and carers to help them develop the confidence to play with their children and enjoy each other's company in a more positive way. Social Services also play a role in Child Protection, and you may sometimes find yourself asked to contribute to a case review with a team of other professionals. All settings and partnerships have their own frameworks and guidelines for Child Protection and you should always be familiar with these and follow the procedures for your authority if you have concerns that a child might be 'at risk'. Most Social Services will also provide you with general advice if you are not sure what to do.

There may be other professionals or teams involved with supporting emotional needs in your particular area such as a Sure Start team or other community-based initiative. Your local Early Years Childcare and Development Partnership should be able to provide you with information about these.

Chapter Seven

Listening to children

Children's opinions and views must be considered valid if we are to include everybody in the educational system in a more democratic and inclusive way. The *SEN Code of Practice* asks us to consider ways in which we can make sure that children are included in their own assessments and planning as far as possible. In this chapter, we explore some of the ways of listening to children.

What would involvement of the *very young* child look like in practice? For younger children, *observation* of what the child is doing can be very helpful. What situations are they happy or sad in? When are they most co-operative or most resistant? What seems to make them anxious or frustrated? With such an observation, it might become possible to interpret what is maintaining a pattern of behaviour or play in a child, and to draw up a hypothesis for what is on the child's own agenda. You will find more ideas to help you observe and assess young children in *The Observation and Assessment of Children in the Early Years* (Mortimer, 2001a), also in this series.

Sometimes we can observe the way children play with 'models' of their world and interpret how they are thinking about it using *small world play*. We can observe the older brother or sister playing in the home corner, acting out considerable feelings of love, anger or fantasy after the arrival of the new baby. It seems that children can usually keep this behaviour distinct and separate from real life and can use it to deal with strong emotions without developing the behaviour at home.

Children's drawings, too, have been used a great deal to help us view a child's state of mind and understanding. They form part of the dialogue we are able to share with them and, therefore, form a springboard for further talking and thinking together. In a similar way, we can use drawings and illustrations as a stimulus for children's own comments and interpretations. What is going on in this picture? Why is the teddy hitting the panda (etc.)? This, too, will give us a glimpse of the way they understand their worlds.

We can use stories and picture books as a means of introducing situations and encouraging children to talk about feelings and behaviours. Early years settings have built up useful collections of stimulus books for covering a range of new situations the child might meet: going to hospital, having a new baby in the family or living with one parent. There are some suggestions of books on page 43.

In a similar way, 'welcome profiles' can be adapted and developed in order to gather information about the child's view on entry into a setting. A welcome profile is a form which parents complete (or an interview which you hold together) gathering information before a child starts in your setting and making parents and child feel welcomed. Open-ended questioning to parents and carers such as: 'Tell me a favourite toy/activity/family outing/ memory'; 'Is there anything that makes your child particularly frightened?'; 'How much help does she need when going to the toilet?'; or 'How does he let you know when he is cross/happy/upset?' This allows you to gather honest information about all children regardless of special need. These questions do not beg a certain reply and license the parent to describe freely the amount of help that might be needed or to celebrate a newfound independence.

There are certain times in a child's life when it becomes more important than ever to 'be there' for them and to listen to what their words, emotions and behaviours are telling you. These are when children go through major life changes, perhaps because of a family breakdown or bereavement. There are some ideas in the next chapter for how you might work to prevent later mental health difficulties and to help the children come to terms with what is happening to them. Research suggests that the best people to provide support when something traumatic happens are the existing supporters in your life and that outside specialist counselling is only needed where, for whatever reason, these systems do not work.

Chapter Eight

Supporting young children through life changes

Talking to young children about family breakdown

Families come in many different shapes and sizes and this is bound to be reflected in both the families and helpers who attend your local setting. At least one in four families in the UK has one parent absent for whatever reason, and in 90% of these families it is the father. About one child in eight is likely to experience family divorce before the age of ten, and about a third of these children are under five. For some of these families, feelings will still be very raw and vulnerable. How can you talk to young children about family breakdown and how can you help them to cope and to express their feelings in the least damaging way?

Young children cannot begin to understand the complexities of adult relationships. They usually accept their family circumstances, arguments and all, as the way things normally are. A family breakdown can take them utterly by surprise and cause misery and bewilderment. Coming just at a time when the parents will be absorbed in their own conflicts and emotions, this can leave the child feeling isolated and even in some way responsible for the split. Their early years setting or care worker might be an important constant at a time when home life is confusing and unsettled. Here, there are grown-ups who have time to give the children special attention at a time when feelings are very muddled. They are not emotionally involved, and they can listen and acknowledge the feelings that the children might be expressing in their play or behaviour.

The children are bound to be feeling miserable. Research has suggested that children rarely see the advantage of their parents living apart, even if there were constant rows. Even if a family split is clearly the only option, children cannot be expected to support that decision in every case. In a sense, there are no 'right answers' from the child's point of view. However, research has also suggested that children adjust best to the change if they continue to feel loved and valued by both parents, even though they live apart. Children whose parents discuss with them what is going on appear to cope better. They need clear information in a way that they can understand. 'Where am I going to live?' 'When will I see Daddy?' 'Is he still my Daddy?' 'Was it because I was naughty?' 'What about Grandpa?' They cannot be expected to support one parent against another, no matter how rejected, angry or guilty the remaining parent feels. They must feel allowed to talk about the missing parent, even if this is distressing for the partner remaining.

For these reasons, it is sometimes easier for the children to talk about their feelings away from home. As a carer, and perhaps friend of the family, it will be helpful for you to gather the facts from the parent, and establish what the child knows. Agree the factual information you may need to give the child, and appoint a particular carer who is going to be giving particular attention to the child. Concentrate on making the child feel secure and comforted during the pre-school session. Help to find words to express what the child is feeling, even if these feelings are coming out as challenging behaviour or particular quietness. Do not force the child to talk, but just be there, close by, as an extra comforter and listener as needed.

Helping children through bereavement and loss

For any of us, coping with a child's bereavement can be as great an emotional challenge as we can meet. All of our own emotions, feelings of inadequacy, perhaps even past bereavements and losses, seem to get in the way. It is important to recognise that this is bound to be so. You will need to support one another at this time, as well as easing the time for a bereaved child. Somewhere around 50 children a day suffer a parental bereavement in this country. For many, this will be their first raw experience of death or loss. Though flooded with television and computer images of violence and death, the characters appear to survive all kinds of drama, or the game reruns with everybody still in tact. Small wonder that young children find it hard to grasp that death is permanent.

Some researchers have described definite stages that children typically move through when they have experienced a bereavement. This can take place in many different orders, and at more than one stage at once, so you will not see a smooth progression as the child 'comes to terms' with the loss. The stages include *shock, anger, sadness* and *rebuilding.*

At the *shock* stage, children appear to be almost denying that the death has occurred. In your setting, you may feel an initial impression that the child is not grieving at all, but, on close inspection, you might see a rather frozen child, moving through play activities and routines on 'automatic control', easily thrown by the unexpected. This stage can last hours, weeks and even months.

Children also typically experience a stage of *anger* where tantrums might be frequent with much blaming of others and a sense of unfairness. Their concentration on playing and joining in might fall, with a far greater emphasis on emotional interaction and who is doing what to whom. This is equivalent to the typical stage of anger in which an adult might be agonising 'Why me?' Young children might find the words very hard to express, and have also been taught not to display aggressive anger onto others; hence a potentially muddling and confusing time. Their closest relatives will be going through similar feelings and may not be as emotionally available and supportive to their child as they would wish to be.

In the stage of *sadness*, the child might be feeling an overwhelming feeling of sorrow and longing. You might find a previously sociable child preferring her own company and appearing sad and listless. You might find her playing long imaginary games which relive the past, and you can expect tearfulness and a need for cuddling and comfort. Life seems to regather some feeling of purpose again at the *rebuilding* stage, on average, towards the end of the first year.

Making a difference
So what can you actually *do* to support a child who has recently been bereaved in your setting? You are in a position to provide the very

continuity and stability that the child needs at this time of change and loss. Do encourage the child back to you at the earliest opportunity, since the atmosphere of 'normality' your setting will give will help greatly. Any bereaved child needs to be reassured that the muddling, changing and very intense feelings he or she is experiencing are normal and acceptable. Your words can help to provide meaning and explanation to some very frightening emotions. Talk to the family to find out more about family life at the present time. You can find out the words that the family have used to explain events, and it will be helpful for you to understand the cultural and religious background to this.

If the child wishes to cry, do allow this – it is absolutely normal and you will be able to find sensitive ways of telling the group why he or she is sad, and what they can do to help too. The child might want to talk about the funeral, or draw pictures of the lost parent. Accept these totally, talk about the memory openly, even if it makes you both sad. Perhaps you can work with the family to build up a special book of memories and photographs, which then becomes something the child can get out whenever she or he wants to talk about her or his loss. Here are some examples of how one might communicate: 'I see you're looking at your photographs; shall we talk about Mummy today?' 'I can see that you are feeling very cross today. That's OK because you've lost a very dear Dad. Let me help you tidy up, then we'll go and say "sorry" to Ahmed together.' 'I can see how sad you are feeling today. I remember feeling very sad and crying a lot when my brother died. Let's sit quietly together for a while.'

Secure base

One of the most positive ways in which you can support a child through major life changes is by providing a secure and familiar base at a time of change and upheaval. Looking back through this book, we discovered key ways in which we can promote children's positive mental health and all these will play a role if you are supporting a vulnerable child. Try to stay calm and positive. Continue to show that you value children for who they are, celebrating diversity and rising to the challenge of any inappropriate behaviour. Try to tune in to what each child is feeling and be aware of the role that your own feelings and emotions are playing as well. Above all, share pleasure and fun together; this is one of the best ways we know of building secure relationships which inspire confidence and positive mental health.

References

Bennathan, M. and Boxhall, M. (2000) *Effective Intervention in Primary Schools – Nurture Groups* (Second Edition). London: David Fulton Publishers.

Bowlby, J. (1998) *A Secure Base: Clinical Implications of Attachment Theory.* London: Routledge.

DfES (2001) *The Special Educational Needs Code of Practice.* Nottingham: DfES Publications.

DfES (2001) *Promoting Children's Mental Health within Early Years and School Settings.* Nottingham: DfES Publications.

Mortimer, H. (1998) *Learning through Play: Circle Time.* Leamington Spa: Scholastic Ltd.

Mortimer, H. (2000a) *The Music Makers Approach: inclusive activities for young children with special educational needs.* Tamworth: NASEN.

Mortimer, H. (2000b) *Developing Individual Behaviour Plans in Early Years Settings.* Tamworth: NASEN.

Mortimer, H. (2001a) *The Observation and Assessment of Children in the Early Years.* Lichfield: QEd Publications.

Mortimer, H. (2001b) *Personal, Social and Emotional Development of Children in the Early Years.* Lichfield: QEd Publications.

Mortimer, H. (2001) *Special Needs and Early Years Provision.* London: Continuum.

Qualifications and Curriculum Authority (QCA) (2000) *Curriculum Guidance for the Foundation Stage.* Hayes: QCA Publications.

Useful resources

Collins, M. (2001) *Circle Time for the Very Young.* Bristol: Lucky Duck Publishing Ltd.

Gardner, H. (1983) *Frames of Mind: The Theory of Multiple Intelligences.* New York: Basic Books.

Henderson, A. (1995) *Behaviour in pre-school groups.* Pre-school Learning Alliance, 69 Kings Cross Road, London WC1X 9LL.

Jenny Mosley Circle Time Kit. Cambridge: LDA (puppets, rainstick, magician's cloak and many props for making circle time motivating).

Lown, J. (2001) *Circle of Friends.* Positive Behaviour Management, 7 Quinton Close, Ainsdale, Merseyside PR8 2TD.

Lown, J. (2002) *Promoting Self-Esteem.* Positive Behaviour Management (see above).

The Magination Press specialises in books that help young children deal with personal or psychological concerns. You can get a catalogue from The Eurospan Group, 3 Henrietta Street, Covent Garden, London WC2E 8LU.

Mayer, J.S. and Salovey, P. (1993) 'The intelligence of emotional intelligence', *Intelligence*, 17, 433–442.

Merrett, F. (1997) *Positive Parenting.* Lichfield: QEd Publications.

Mortimer, H. (1998) *Personal and Social Development.* Leamington Spa: Scholastic.

Mosley, J. (1993) *Turn your school around.* Cambridge: LDA.

Mosley, J. (1998) *More Quality Circle Time.* Cambridge: LDA.

Mosley, J. and Sonnet, H. (2001) *Here We Go Round – Quality Circle Time for 3–5 year-olds*. Trowbridge: Positive Press Ltd.

Salovey, P. and Sluyter, D.J. (1997) *Emotional Development and Emotional Intelligence*. New York: Basic Books.

Stenhouse, G. (1994) *Confident Children: Developing Your Child's Self-Esteem*. Oxford: Oxford University Press.
Stockton-on-Tees Educational Psychology Service (2001) *Managing your 4–8 year-old*. Lichfield: QEd Publications.

Vine, P. and Todd, T. (2001) *Ring of Confidence – A Quality Circle Time Programme to Support Personal Safety for the Foundation Stage*. Trowbridge: Positive Press Ltd.

Organisations and support groups

Barnardo's: provides care and support for children in need and their families, with projects throughout the UK.
Barnardo's, Tanners Lane, Barkingside, Ilford, Essex IG6 1QG
Tel: 020 8550 8822
Web site: www.barnardos.org.uk

The CaF Directory of specific conditions and rare syndromes in children (including those that affect behaviour) with their family support networks can be obtained on subscription from Contact a Family, Equity House, 209–211 City Road, London EC1V 1JN

Children's Society: works with children in need and their families, for example, in independent living projects for children leaving care and home – finding projects for children with special needs. Runs several family centres and parenting projects.
Children's Society, Edward Rudolf House, Margery Street, London WC1X 0JL
Tel: 020 7841 4400 (Helpline: 020 7841 4436)
Web site: www.the-childrens-society.org.uk

Department for Education and Skills (DfES), Sanctuary Buildings, Great Smith Street, London SW1P 3BT
Tel: 0870 000 2288   Fax: 01928 794248   Email: info@dfes.gov.uk
Web site: www.dfes.gov.uk

The National Association for Special Educational Needs (NASEN), 4/5 Amber Business Village, Amber Close, Tamworth B77 4RP
Tel: 01827 311500   Fax: 01827 313005   Email: welcome@nasen.org.uk
Web site: www.nasen.org.uk

National Children's Bureau (NCB): a multidisciplinary organisation concerned with the promotion and identification of the interests of all children and young people. Involved in research, policy and practice development, and consultancy.
NCB, 8 Wakley Street, London EC1V 1NG
Tel: 020 7843 6000   Fax: 020 7278 9512
Web site: www.ncb.org.uk

National Council of Voluntary Child Care Organisations: umbrella group for voluntary organisations dealing with children. Ensuring the well-being and safeguarding of children and families and maximising the voluntary sector's contribution to the provision of services.
NCVCCO, Unit 4, Pride Court, 80–82 White Lion Street, London N1 9PF
Tel: 020 7833 3319
Web site: www.ncvcco.org.uk

National Society for the Prevention of Cruelty to Children: for training on SEN, child protection and family work.
NSPCC, National Training Centre, 3 Gilmour Close, Beaumont Leys, Leicester LE4 1EZ

National NEWPIN: voluntary organisation working with families to help break the cycle of destructive family behaviour.
NEWPIN, Sutherland House, 35 Sutherland Square, Walworth, London SE17 3EE
Tel: 020 7358 5900
Web site: www.newpin.org.uk

PIPPIN (Parents in Partnership – Parent Infant Network): a national charity whose main aim is to maintain and improve the emotional help of families.
PIPPIN, Derwood, Todds Green, Stevenage SG1 2JE
Web site: www.pippin.org.uk

Pre-school Learning Alliance, 69 Kings Cross Road, London WC1X 9LL
Tel: 020 7833 0991   Fax: 020 7837 4942
Web site: www.pre-school.org.uk

Qualifications and Curriculum Authority (QCA), 83 Piccadilly, London
W1J 8QA
Tel: 020 7509 5555   Fax: 020 7509 6666
Web site: www.qca.org.uk

QEd Publications, The Rom Building, Eastern Avenue, Lichfield, Staffs.
WS13 6RN
Tel: 01543 416353   Fax: 01543 419144   Email: orders@qed.uk.com
Web site: www.qed.uk.com

Save the Children: works in the UK and overseas with children, young
people and their families experiencing disadvantage and discrimination. In
the UK, concerned with developing policy and practice in partnership with
statutory and voluntary organisations.
Save the Children, Mary Datchelor House, 17 Grove Lane, London SE5
8RD
Tel: 020 7703 5400
Web site: www.savethechildren.org.uk